I'm delighted to own this beautiful book! I've followed *#Niteblessings* on social media for some time and whilst in hospital chaplaincy ministry, I've read them to many of my patients who have found tremendous comfort in the words. As I read through this book, I am giving thanks for the tender words that encourage and bless me too!

Revd Ann Stevenson

#Niteblessings are life savers! They speak right into the depths of my heart. Hardly a day goes by when I am not calmed and soothed by these beautiful words.

Sally Ide, teacher, hospital volunteer, nanny, mother

More #Niteblessings . . . is a beautiful book with words that calm and encourage as you read and are reminded of God's grace and love for each and every one of us.

Chris Mercer-Turner, international
gospel artist and Anglican ordinand

These are brilliant wee prayers that help some of us who keep asking the Lord Jesus – Lord teach us how to pray!

John K. Brown

Short, sharp, to-the-point, a beautiful meditation/reflection for morning or night. *#Niteblessings* enables you to step away from the busyness of life and soak refreshingly in God's presence.

Kerry Parry, community chaplain, Australia

MORE #Niteblessings

Further meditations for the end of the day

LION

Published by
Lion Hudson Limited
Wilkinson House, Jordan Hill Business Park
Banbury Road, Oxford OX2 8DR, England
www.lionhudson.com/lion

ISBN 978 0 74598 091 1
e-ISBN 978 0 74598 092 8

First edition 2019

Acknowledgments

Scripture quotations taken from The Holy Bible, English Standard Version® (ESV®)

Copyright © 2001 by Crossway, a publishing ministry of Good News Publishers.

All rights reserved.

Extracts from the following songs:

p178 "Immanuel, O Immanuel" Graham Kendrick © 1988 grahamkendrick.co.uk

p180 "Meekness and Majesty" Copyright © 1986 Thankyou Music (Adm. by
CapitolCMGPublishing.com excl. UK & Europe, adm. By Integrity Music, part of the
David C. Cook family, songs@integritymusic.com)

p181 "You Laid Aside your Majesty" Copyright © 1985 Thankyou Music (Adm. by
CapitolCMGPublishing.com excl. UK & Europe, adm. By Integrity Music, part of the
David C. Cook family, songs@integritymusic.com

p185 "The Candle Song" Graham Kendrick © 1988 grahamkendrick.co.uk

A catalogue record for this book is available from the British Library

Printed and bound in Serbia, August 2019, LH55

This volume of *#Niteblessings* is dedicated to Joel, Jake, Marion, and Dave Brown, whose courage and strength in the face of extreme trial have been amazing. I thank God for you all.

It is also dedicated to my children – Riodhna, Anna, Benjamin, and Matthew – and to my wife, Debbie. I thank God for you all and am more grateful than you could ever imagine that I have the privilege of sharing life with you.

Lastly, the book is dedicated to my church family at Dundonald Elim Church. What God is doing among us is amazing. Thank you for the privilege of leading you. You are never far from my thoughts when I write these blessings.

Acknowledgements

Writing can be a lonely experience – there are many days when you are locked away from the world with no one physically present other than God. Yet it is also always a community affair. There are always others' voices in your head and in your heart as you write. That is because writing must always, in the end, be an exercise in partnership, working with others, learning from them, relying on them, listening to them, and being shaped by them.

My deep thanks go to all those people whose company helps me shape my blessing each day. First, the community of Dundonald Elim Church: working with this leadership team, staff team, and church family is a wonderful blessing. The privilege of being allowed to walk with you at some of the most difficult junctions in your lives always amazes me and I am blessed beyond measure by your love, prayers, and support – thank you.

I am also deeply grateful to the many people with whom I have walked over the years and with whom I am blessed to still be involved. Often when you pastor a church, you can feel that you only matter to the church when you are there. That is, of course, an inevitability (and perhaps a cost) of pastoral ministry. Yet there are others with whom your connection continues. It weaves and changes into the fabric of your life in beautiful ways. That means I am deeply thankful to all those who have given me permission to pastor them over the years, whether we are still in contact or not – your presence in my life has enriched my deeply – but I am particularly thankful to those with whom I continue to walk, in one way or another, from the many years of ministry I have been blessed to have. Thank you for your continued prayers, support, love, encouragement, and letting me be part of what God is doing through #Niteblessings in so many peoples' lives day by day.

I am grateful to all at Lion Hudson for their support, understanding, and patience with me. To Jon Oliver, Suzanne Wilson-Higgins, Louise Titley, and the whole team of designers, marketers, graphics specialists, publicists, and support staff – thank you.

I am grateful to you, the reader, and to those who continue to bless others with #Niteblessings, in both their book form and on social media. Thank you for making this amazing adventure of blessing possible and for continuing to share your stories. A particular thank you to those who are pastors and leaders themselves, who use these blessings in their roles as pastors, chaplains, encouragers, life-group leaders, and in so many other ways.

Lastly, and most importantly, I am deeply grateful to God, the great blesser. The One who loves us, walks with us, and sustains us. Without Him, I am nothing. He is, beyond the shadow of a doubt, the greatest blessing of my life.

Soli Deo Gloria

Malcolm Duncan
County Down
July 2019

Contents

Foreword

When the first volume of *#Niteblessings* was released in November 2018, I was profoundly touched by the messages from people who were helped by it. It quickly became clear to both my publisher and to me that these simple blessings were reaching people in the most amazing ways. We were astounded at how God was using #Niteblessings to help people facing some of the most difficult circumstances you could imagine. I had some idea of the ways in which they were used from the responses that I receive on social media to the Niteblessing I write each evening, but I was genuinely moved by the messages that started flooding in. I received messages from men and women who were facing terminal illnesses, people who had lost loved ones, young people searching for a sense of direction, teenagers struggling with thoughts of self-harming, brothers and sisters in Christ who were battling mental illnesses, and scores of other situations. Many were being helped to find a way back to faith, a pathway home to the loving and tender arms of their Creator. A lot of people have become Christians through reading these little blessings.

Others have told me of how they have bought the book as a gift for loved ones, friends, and colleagues and been amazed at how God has used them. For all these reasons and many more, we felt that a second edition, *More #Niteblessings*, would be a good idea. So here it is.

None of the blessings contained in this edition are in the first volume of the book. There is a very simple reason for that: each one is written fresh every day. I have often been asked if I write a lot of the blessings together and then use a publishing tool for social media to help manage their appearance on platforms such as Twitter, Facebook, and Instagram. The answer is that I do not. The birthing of each blessing is a simple process. I take a few moments each day (normally between 9.30 and 10.00 p.m.) to reflect on the day and to craft the blessing. I then find an image that I think captures the blessing I have written and post them together on my various social media platforms. Each blessing is like fresh bread for that day. I am then deeply moved as I see how many people read them, share them, like them, and comment on them.

There is something inherently beautiful and life-giving, I think, in blessing others. It somehow roots us in the soil that God intends. Speaking good over one another, reminding one another of the goodness of our Creator and our Saviour, is a positive trait and habit, don't you think? And somehow, in a mysterious way, when we open our lives to share a blessing or to receive one, much more becomes possible in our lives. The gifts of hope, faith, thankfulness, and joy are somehow experienced, even in the darkest and most difficult of circumstances.

#Niteblessings seems to particularly resonate with those for whom life is currently hard. Perhaps it is because the blessings are short and can therefore be read easily. Perhaps it is because they capture something of the reality of faith when times are hard and circumstances are uncertain. Perhaps it is because the blessings can be shared with the confidence that they are deeply rooted in Scripture and in what Scripture tells us about the character and love of God. Perhaps it is because they can be shared with those who find reading the Bible hard or somehow uncomfortable. Whatever the reason, I am

grateful to God for the fact that these blessings seem to be helping people. I pray they will help you too. And that you will use them to help and bless others.

I continue to post a blessing each night on social media on the following dedicated platforms:

Twitter: @Niteblessing

Facebook: @Niteblessings

Instagram: Niteblessings

In addition, I continue to share and reflect on the blessings on my own social media platforms:

Twitter: @MalcolmJDuncan

Facebook: RevMalcolmDuncan

Instagram: MalcolmJDuncan

Blog: MalcolmDuncan.org

Website: MalcolmDuncan.co.uk

I would be delighted to engage with you via one of them. Please take a look if you can. Or get in touch directly via email – malcolm@dundonaldelim.church – as I would love to hear about some of the ways in which God is using these blessings. If I can help you in any way, then please contact me.

As we look ahead, we are working on a range of other blessings. Just two are "LifeBlessings", which are daily blessings for different seasons of life, and "SoulSongs", which are blessings and reflections based on the Psalms. Our prayer is that they will be used by God to strengthen, encourage, and inspire you to continue in your faith, and to discover the beauty and grace of the God who fashioned you, walks with you, and offers you life.

May God continue to remind us of the many blessings we enjoy in our lives because of His extravagant love and mercy.

Soli Deo Gloria

Malcolm Duncan
County Down
July 2019

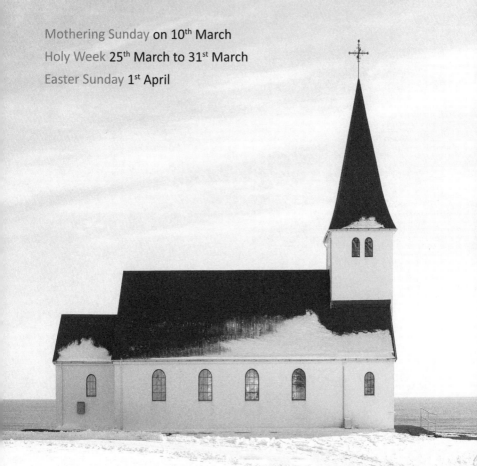

Looking for Niteblessings for specific festivals?
You will find them for:

Mothering Sunday on 10th March
Holy Week 25th March to 31st March
Easter Sunday 1st April

January

1st January Each day of this year may you find delight in simple blessings: a new dawn every morning, the gift of being alive, and above all the beautiful, inexplicable grace of God that sees you, loves you, and offers you an embrace of welcome and acceptance that can never be broken.

2nd January May your heart be shielded by nail-pierced hands of love; may your sorrow be buried at the cross; may hope blossom for you at the entrance to an empty tomb.

3rd January Let your soul sing to the Spirit's tune: a beautiful harmony of grace, hope, and joy; and if you have lost your desire to raise your voice to the music of heaven, may God bring the notes of eternity to you once again. Sing – you are alive and there is hope.

4th January May the first coming of Christ root you in grace, mercy, and forgiveness, and may His promised return keep hope, expectation, and joy alive in your soul. May the light of the world "eclipse the gloomy clouds of night" and see "death's dark shadows put to flight".

5th January May the rumour take root, may the whisper grow louder, may the light blaze brightly in your soul that God has come to us in Christ! He has conquered death, He has overcome despair, He has not only brought hope, He is the loving hope of all who turn to Him.

6th January May your capacity to love be greater than your capacity to hate; your ability to forgive deeper than your deepest hurt. May you see others as God sees them, and may your responses reflect His mercy, love, and truth to others. May you know that you are loved by Him.

7th January You live on a visited planet where the Creator became the Crucified because of love. Even the ground beneath your feet and the air you breathe will one day be transformed. God will make all things new. May this hope galvanize your soul and give you courage.

8th January Nothing takes God by surprise. Whatever you are facing tonight, He is able to carry you through uncertainty, fear, sorrow, and grief. May you know His presence reassuring you, His power carrying you, and His promises sustaining you always.

9th January May you be given the gift of thankfulness: for blessings, memories, joy, and love. Lay your disappointments and sadnesses at the foot of the cross, remembering that absence is proof of a presence you have loved and enjoyed. You cannot miss what you never had.

10th January May Christ's hope hold you tightly. Remember that He is close enough to know what you feel and face, strong enough to protect you and keep you safe, and faithful enough to finish what He has begun in you. May today's moments be sculpted into possibilities for tomorrow.

11th January May the constancy of God's love and grace carry you through everything you face. May your eyes be firmly fixed on Jesus, your heart be shielded in His loving hands, and your identity be firmly rooted in Him. May His voice be clearest and His smile most important to you.

12th January Remember that goodness and mercy watch over God's people. No matter how deep the valley or how dark the night, He is your shepherd and never abandons you. May you know His nearness and protection, and always listen for His loving voice above the noise of others.

13th January Remember that each word of your life is known to God. He is present at every paragraph's transition; there at the end and start of every chapter; present for the opening sentence and there at the very end. He has the last word, knows you, loves you, and upholds you.

14th January Whether today has held sadness or joy for you, may you know peace, stillness, and grace in your soul tonight. If you feel excitement at what the future holds, may it be protected and nurtured. If you feel fear and dread, may they be replaced with faith and hope.

15th January May you be refreshed by rest, strengthened by the Spirit, and blessed by the Father's embrace. Tonight as you sleep, may the day's weariness be washed away and may you be given new hope and determination for what lies ahead, alive to the possibilities of another day.

16th January May you remember that there is always hope. No matter what has happened today, whether you feel elated or defeated; if the last twenty-four hours have been marked with faith or with fear; if you sense God is near or feel distant from Him, may you be rooted in hope.

17th January May you step into the new day tomorrow with fresh energy and purpose in your stride. May you be given the grace to know that God is bigger than your circumstances. May you have the courage to let your struggles refine you but never define you – they too will pass.

18th January May God give you rest, may His Spirit give you hope, and may you embrace the forgiveness and mercy that His Son offers. He is present in your life, knows what you have faced, and is able to transform the darkest situations and bring light and grace for tomorrow.

19th January May you find a rhythm of rest amid what sometimes feels like the chaos of life. May your heart be held gently by God, your mind be stilled by His mercy, and your soul be soothed by His Spirit. May you turn your gaze to the One who always loves you and always knows you.

20th January May the deep and settled peace of God rest on you like a warm blanket of love and grace. May you feel the safety of His covering and the security of His protection.

21st January May you sense a stirring of possibility in your soul; a seed of hope planted by God that grows into something so beautiful that it graces your life forever. May its flower release a scent of grace that diffuses through every aspect of your life and brings you peace.

22nd January May God give you rest, His Spirit give you hope, and may you embrace the forgiveness and mercy that His Son offers. He is present in your life, knows what you have faced, and is able to transform the darkest situations and bring light and grace for tomorrow.

23rd January God never abandons us. He holds us through storms even when we do not feel His arms; sets sentinels to guard us from far more than we can realize this side of heaven; hears our cries and feels our heartbreaks. We can trust Him even when we do not understand Him.

24th January If the soil of your soul is shredded by uncertainty, fear, or sadness, may you have grace to remember that God plants seeds of possibility in the furrows left by the blades of life. From them grow new plants of hope, because His hand is never lifted from the plough.

25th January At the end of your day, you may have come to the end of yourself. May God grant you new strength, new grace, and new hope. Strength to admit your weakness and lean into Him. Grace to trust Him with the moments of this day. Hope to believe that He will not let you go.

26th January Take a breath. As you do, may you breathe in a sense of God's proximity, His closer-than-a-brother nearness, His indwelling intimacy. May your breathing out be long and gentle, a sigh releasing your fear and frustration into the hands of your Father. All is well.

27th January Tonight may you know the gentleness of a Saviour who hides you under the shadow of His wing; the comfort of a Father who knows what it feels like to lose someone He loves; and the promise of a God who assures you that He will never leave you nor forsake you.

28th January May you remember tonight that God is worth it all. He can be trusted with your deepest fears, is the source of your ultimate strength, the provider of all the grace you need, and the object of all your hopes and longings. May you find yourself in Him.

29th January May God lift the heaviness of your heart and give you a lightness in your step; may He break your shackles of anxiety and help you walk in freedom; may He lift the stoop of your pressures and give you a posture of possibility.

30th January May you find freedom in frailty and a sense of release in the reality that you do not have to hold it all together. God holds you in the midst of the darkest nights. His comfort carries you even when you cannot feel it. He is holding you in the midst of the trial.

31st January May you know the beauty of being yourself, with all of your vulnerabilities. You have nothing to hide from God and He doesn't need you to pretend. This is true freedom – the freedom to be yourself, honestly and openly before God, knowing that you are loved and held.

February

1st February May God envelop you in a blanket of grace, surround you with an atmosphere of love, and remind you that no matter how dark your day has been, He is the source of light, life, and hope. May your deepest fears be absorbed by His deeper grace and constant love.

2nd February As one day ends and another begins, may you be given the grace to remember that all things pass. May the weariness of the day that is ending be lifted from your body and your soul, and may you be given new energy and new strength for another day.

3rd February Whether today has held joy or sorrow, may you know the comfort of a Father who loves you more than you could ever hope, and who knows exactly how you feel tonight. He walks with you always, even when it feels as though He is walking in silence.

4th February No matter what happens in your life, may there always be hope. Who you are is held by God. May you be given the gift of faith tonight: a profound and simple sense that God loves you and that He is able to carry you through anything you face and give you strength.

5th February Remember that God always finishes what He starts, even though you might feel that your future is uncertain or that His purposes in you are fragile and incomplete. He will finish His work in you, presenting you faultless. May you have grace to keep going, no matter what.

6th February Remember that to love and be loved, you must be vulnerable. If you feel the pain of vulnerability, may you also know that it is a pathway to being truly alive, even when it hurts. May you know the wonder of being fully loved by God and be able to love Him in return.

7th February May you experience the gift of kind words tomorrow, given or received. May you somehow be reminded that God knows you, loves you, and is for you and not against you; and may you use your words to give someone else hope, show them kindness, and celebrate their value.

8th February If you are apprehensive about the road ahead, may you be given the grace to see possibilities rather than problems. May the twists and turns fill you with excitement and adventure rather than stress and uncertainty. May your view of tomorrow lead you to be hopeful.

9th February May your grief be tempered by God's comfort and may your heartache be soothed by His grace. In the midst of your uncertainty and sadness, may God be your security and joy. As life takes you through a valley, may you catch a glimpse of the Son.

10th February May God untangle the strands of your soul. If life has confused you, may the giver of life bring peace. May He weave the threads of who you are into the most beautiful tapestry, bound by beauty and dyed in grace, and may He give you strength in the midst of your mess.

11th February May the life that flows from God's love root you in hope. Your identity is not defined by your circumstances or emotions, or the attitudes of others. Remember that your worth and dignity are rooted in God's view of you. You are cherished, loved, accepted, and forgiven.

12th February Receive the gift of letting go by giving God sorrows that you cannot bear, fears that you should not carry, and hurts that have weighed you down. May you release everything in your hands into God's care, holding open palms before Him. To be empty-handed is to be free.

13th February Snowdrops beginning to push through the earth remind us that winter will soon pass and spring will come again. May you know the Spirit's life stirring in you, even if it feels as if winter has gripped your soul. Life is stronger than death, hope greater than despair.

14th February On a day when love is often made to feel gaudy and cheap, remember that you are loved as you are, not as you should be. God loves the broken you, the honest you, the messed up you. His love is deep enough to accept you and strong enough to perfect you one day.

15th February Life is fragile, strong, beautiful. Much of it lies beyond our control; we can pass from now into eternity in a moment. Beauty, love, ugliness, and hate all lie within our hearts, yet life's beauty is breathtaking. May you know God's presence in the midst of life always.

16th February Each day brings a blank page upon which will be written joys or sorrows, hopes or fears. Whether your life's words today brought good news or bad, were expected or not, may you know that the author of life is faithful and able to carry you through every chapter.

17th February May grace carry you through every trial, and comfort you through every heartbreak. May God's nearness soothe your soul tonight. Those you love are safe in His care. May you take the outstretched hand of God and find in His offered love a new beginning.

18th February God knows your name. He understands your story. Nothing that you have faced has gone unnoticed. Tonight, He offers you His presence as a gift and His promise as your hope. May you let Him walk with you as a friend, tonight and always.

19th February Amid the demands you face, may God's voice be clearest, may His invitation be most important, and may His gaze catch your eye. As you face the challenges of living well and loving deeply, may you discover the abundant supply of His strength and grace for your life.

20th February May you know the presence of God in this season of your life. As you think about your past, may He bring a sense of completion. As you think about your present, may He bring peace. As you think about your future, may He bring hope.

21st February As one day ends, may you know rest at the deepest level of your soul. May God bring you physical restoration, spiritual renewal, and emotional resilience. May your heart be laden with grace, your spirit lightened by hope, and your mind stilled by God's enduring grace.

22nd February Whatever today has held for you, may you know tonight that God holds you. Nothing is beyond His seeing or knowing. He has been with you at the lowest moments of your life and at the highest, and His love for you remains undiminished. May this truth bring you peace.

23rd February May you find beauty in the most unexpected places of your life. In the midst of disappointment, may you find the gift of new beginnings; in the midst of heartache, may you discover how deeply you can love; in the midst of trouble, may you be given the gift of faith.

24th February May the dawn of another day remind you of God's unceasing faithfulness. Troubles pass and joy comes in the morning. Your life may not be what you thought it would be, for better or worse, but remember that nothing takes God by surprise. He is there, because He always is.

25th February May your soul sing for joy and your spirit lift in praise because of this one truth: you are loved more deeply than you could ever imagine. God knows the deepest secrets of your heart and is committed to finishing the work He has begun in you. Don't give up!

26th February May your worries for the future be lifted from your heart and held in God's gracious hands. There is always uncertainty about tomorrow and we can never be the masters of our own fate, but may you remember that God can be trusted with your deepest fears.

27th February May you know God's strengthening as you rest. May He replace all you gave today, and as you rise tomorrow, may you do so with a fresh sense of purpose, direction, and determination. The events of today cannot be changed; your decisions about tomorrow are yet to be made.

28th February May you remember that you are not alone. If you find yourself feeling isolated and longing for companionship, may God grant you the desire of your heart, but may you also remember that He is with you. He sees every tear, hears every sigh. He is present in every moment.

29th February May you be graced with space. An extra day is a rare gift. As you reflect on the presence of this day in your diary, may you be reminded of the gift of each moment. May you pause in the presence of God and be thankful for simple things – friends, family and faith.

March

1ˢᵗ March May you know the security of God's grace. There is nothing you need to prove, nowhere you need to hide, nothing you need to earn and no one you need to impress. God, all-present, all-knowing, all-seeing, all-powerful, extends a hand of grace to you. Take it and live.

2ⁿᵈ March In life's unpredictability, may God be the steady hand on your tiller. Remember that He understands your uncertainty and stands able to give you stability, peace, and direction. He is your peace amid crashing waves, your shelter in storms, and your comfort in chaos.

3ʳᵈ March May you see further with your soul than you do through your natural eyes. May the promises of God be the lenses through which you view the world. May the rags of your failures and fears be lifted from your shoulders, and may hope and possibility be your new mantle.

4th March May the grace of God rise upon you and bring you hope and courage. May His mercy flood your heart and His hope saturate your soul. May joy be your companion, and comfort be your constant friend. May you always remember that you are never alone.

5th March May you always remember that God is bigger than all of your circumstances, stronger than any opposition you face, better than any of your best aspirations, and more loving than anyone who has ever loved or will ever love you. May He be your hope, life, and joy always.

6th March May God's grace lift you out of the doldrums of despair, the forebodings of fear, and the snares of sorrow. May it push you out of the confines of comfort zones, the destructiveness of other people's definitions of you, and the isolation that insecurity brings. May you live a life freed by grace.

7th March May you be given the grace to open your hands rather than clench your fists; may you be given the humility to kneel in weakness rather than stand in defiance; may you be given the courage to be vulnerable rather than shut off from others; may God be your hope.

8th March May you find faith to welcome change instead of fearing it, the whisper of what might be louder in your imagination than the shouts of complacency or false comfort. May the murmurings of possibility in your soul join God's song of grace. He has more for your life.

9th March May you be given the gift of trusting: that you can leave today, with all of its accomplishments and frustrations, in God's hands; that, somehow, your whole journey will one day make sense; that your tomorrows are held in the hands of a God who is faithful – always.

10th March For mourning mums and those who miss their mums – comfort; for mums who feel like failures and those they let down – grace; for those who yearn to be mums and those who know they never will be – peace; for blessed mums – joy; for mums who have trusted someone else with their child – peace.

11th March May God sustain you in the desert.
May His mercy upon you be like refreshing rain amid
dryness, His presence shielding you from the heat
of the day, His promises acting like a guiding star as
you travel onward. In the sandstorm, may He be your
shield. He is enough.

12th March May God bring fresh clarity to your
vision; may you understand yourself as loved and
forgiven by Him; may your view of the future be
refracted through the lens of His grace and mercy;
may your memories of the past be diffused by His
tender care and compassion.

13th March Remember that when people reject you,
God never does. When you are disempowered, God is
always your strength. When your life is shattered by
the actions of others, God makes beautiful things from
the broken pieces. He knows, He sees, and He loves
you.

14th March May you stand steady in the midst of the gale, your life deeply rooted in the character of God, your resolve strengthened by His promises, and your actions shaped by integrity and grace. May you remember that you are never alone – God is present even if He is silent.

15th March May your soul sing to heaven's melody; may the signature key of your daily life be grace; may the words you speak be like notes of mercy and truth; and may your actions, attitudes, and responses always be kept in step with hope by the power of the Holy Spirit.

16th March May the peace of God rest upon you tonight like a cloak of protection and strength, giving you a deep sense of well-being, a profound experience of hope, and an assurance of being held and shielded in the arms of Almighty God.

17th March May we each be given the grace to say goodbye when the time is right. Through tears of sadness and joy, may God come close, uniting our hearts in love and giving us grace to love one another tightly and hold one another lightly. There is a season for everything.

18th March May you be given the grace to rest under the protection and restoration of Almighty God tonight. May you rise tomorrow to a fresh day, with thankfulness and hope in your heart. May you know that God goes ahead of you, soothes your soul, and gives you grace.

19th March If you are weary, may you find your rest in God; if you are anxious, may you find your peace in Christ; if you are sad at what you have left, may you find your joy in the God who promises new things ahead. As you step into what is next, may the Spirit give you faith.

20th March May you experience a life of possibility, creativity, joy, and forgiveness that flows from God. May your disappointments be few and your encouragements many. May you hear the loving voice of God whispering your name and speaking hope into the centre of your soul.

21st March May you be given the gift of an open heart, mind, and hands: an open heart to receive God's grace and mercy, an open mind to see the best in people and be able to grow, and open hands so that God can take things that may not matter and give you faith and hope.

22nd March May you be given the gift of being restored tonight: the weariness of today replaced with strength and hope for tomorrow. May your successes and failures be exchanged for the unconditional acceptance and grace of God. You have nothing to prove to your Father.

23rd March In the light of the cross, may you be given the gift of faith. May you see how much God loves you through what Jesus did for you, understand how much Christ has done for you through His death and resurrection, and experience the comfort and assurance of God's Spirit.

24th March May the burdens of the day be lifted by the strong arms of God; may the worries of the day be wiped away by the tender hands of God; may the disappointments of the day be carried by the loving heart of God. May you know the gifts of faith, hope, and love for tomorrow.

25th March As another day ends, may you have the grace to see Jesus for who He is – your Saviour and King – and the humility to lay your life before Him in worship and trust, like those who laid their cloaks before Him on the road to Jerusalem. May you always know that He loves you.

26th March May you discover God's relentless love for you. He breaks through every barrier, challenges every prejudice, dismisses every religious assumption, to reach you. The One who drove moneychangers out and overturned their tables, reaches out His hand of love and grace to you.

27th March If your faith hangs by a thread, may you remember that its strength is determined by God's commitment to you and not by your commitment to Him. May the indestructible gossamer of grace remind you that God is faithful. This Holy Week, may holy hope grip your soul.

28th March May you have the grace, humility, and courage to let Jesus wash your feet. As the Saviour serves you, may you discover in His mercy, compassion, and love keys that release you to new life. Mercy releases kindness, compassion releases hope, and love releases acceptance.

29th March God's love for you is so deep that the Father, Son, and Spirit endured the cross. Receive the gift of faith to embrace new life that flows from the cross and the empty tomb. Embrace the gift of a cleansed conscience, forgiven heart, hopeful future, and empowered life.

30th March Find forgiveness at the cross; catch a glimpse of God's breathtaking love as the Saviour breathes His last; be comforted by the cry of Christ: "It is finished"; discover the depth of God's mercy in Jerusalem's dirt. He has borne your sin – you need carry it no more.

31st March Waiting is never wasted. In the midst of life's uncertainties, with life shrouded in unanswered questions and mystery, may you find the gift of God's silent presence. Your sense of His absence is evidence of His missed presence – a presence that is as sure of

April

1st April The victory of the resurrection reaches into the very centre of your soul and pours in comfort for sorrow. May you feel new life's power at this very moment; in today's reality, may the risen Christ whisper in your soul, "This is not the end of the story. The best is yet to be."

2nd April Remember that God knows you inside and out. He understands your deepest regrets, knows your profoundest fears, and sees the possibilities that lie ahead of you. Rest in the reality of His grace tonight and experience His peace and presence profoundly in your soul.

3rd April May you have the humility to see yourself honestly, as God sees you: loved, cherished, accepted, forgiven, flawed, broken, and in constant need of grace, mercy, and patience. May you walk in confidence and humility, and reject arrogance or false self-deprecation.

4th April May you know the beauty of God's grace restoring your relationship and giving you the gift of hope again. May your heart be held lovingly and tenderly in the hands of God, and may you remember that the One who flung stars into space shields you and guards your soul.

5th April If your soul is downcast, may the Holy Spirit give you hope. If your heart is broken, may the broken Saviour restore you. If you have lost your way, may the way, the truth, and the life lead you back to the right path. If you are facing a battle, may God be your shield.

6th April May you be captivated by what is possible, and liberated from fear of failure. May God give you courage to step into a new future, embraced by His grace, laced with His love, drenched with His joy, saturated by His Spirit, and drawn by a new destiny of faith and hope.

7th April God give you rest, lifting weariness from your soul and tiredness from your body. May He renew your mind, giving you space to think and enliven your spirit by giving you room to breathe. May His strength give you confidence and may you have courage to face tomorrow.

8th April Hope comes in unexpected ways: a child's smile, a sunrise, a still ocean. It also comes in mysteries: walking through sorrow, surviving an enemy's attacks, and in the gifts of absence and crucibles of suffering. May you always be held by hope, whatever you are facing.

9th April May you be drawn forward by hope, not backward by despair. May you be given grace to let sadness, disappointment, and failure fall from your hands at His feet, offering empty hands to God so He can give you faith, taking your hand to lead you into what lies ahead.

10th April May you be reminded that you do not need to stumble about in the darkness anymore. God has given light and hope through His Son Jesus. However far away you feel, may God remind you that you are only a prayer away from home, where He waits to embrace you again.

11th April To believe in God when the sun shines is simple, but to trust Him when darkness shrouds your life requires courage. If your days are filled with light, may you enjoy the warmth of His blessing. If your days are dark, may God give you courage and grace. He is there.

12th April May you be given the gift of peace. The God who has wept with you; who has guarded you in a thousand ways that you will only know in eternity; who has held you as you beat His chest in anger or gripped His hand in fear – He is and always will be here. May this give you peace.

13th April Some moments in our lives feel full of possibility and others feel full of uncertainty. The line between these two perspectives is as slender as the direction of our gaze. At this moment, may your eyes be lifted toward heaven and may uncertainty become possibility.

14th April May faith, hope, and love be worn in your life like a necklace of grace. Faith for assurance that God is present when you do not sense Him. Hope to sustain you in the darkest days. Love so you can rest in God's acceptance of you and love others unconditionally.

15th April May tonight bring restoration and renewal. As you sleep, may God prepare you for tomorrow by strengthening your soul and giving you fresh courage to live bravely and boldly. May your eyes and heart be attentive to each moment and may your spirit sing in hopefulness.

16th April May you release the stresses and strains of today. May your fear and frustrations be carried by the strong arms of God. May you place all the things that you wanted to do but did not accomplish into His care, trusting Him for the strength for all that tomorrow requires.

17th April God has promised that He is close to the broken-hearted and saves those who are crushed in spirit. May you know the reality of this promise tonight. God is near. May His presence heal your broken heart and cause your crushed spirit to blossom into life again.

18th April May you know the gift of faith tonight: to trust that what you face now is not the end of the story; to take the first step into a new season of life, even if you do not know where that journey might lead you; and to find the courage to face your fears and grow.

19th April Uncertainty is only "not knowing" in different clothes. If it is in our hands, then it is a cage that confines us. In God's hands, it is a key that opens a door to new possibilities. May you see it as a key and may it unlock a sense of hopeful anticipation in you.

20th April May the nearness of God's Spirit bring assurance that the darkness will lift, the dawn will come, and light will rise in your heart again. No matter how alone you feel, no matter how uncertain your sense of God, He is closer than your breath and holds you always.

21st April You cannot flourish when you are rooted in fear, so may your soul be planted in the soil of faith and may hope bud on the branches of your life. When you have come to the end of yourself, God is still there. When you feel that you are at a dead end, may God make a way.

22nd April As one day ends and another begins, may you be aware of God's promises: He is good and His love endures forever. May you leave today in God's hands: regrets about what you would change and satisfaction at what has gone well. Peace is your portion, and grace your guard.

23rd April May you plot a new path in a new season. As spring buds at last, may new possibilities bud in you. Where there have been no signs of life, may hope push through. May God plough new furrows in the soil of your soul and may the seed of His word be planted there.

24th April May you find the gift of space: stop and take stock, catch your breath, collect your thoughts. May God help you weigh things up and make good choices, rooted in what brings spiritual, emotional, and physical health. May this moment be a wide and open space for you.

25th April May you learn the art of resting. There is always more for you to do, but you do not need to strive. Let your rest be rooted in satisfaction and not exhaustion. Allow God to lift the weight of weariness from your body and soul; let His life flow through you daily.

26th April May you remember that the hands that flung stars into space are stretched out to you. Scarred hands, a reminder that God knows your pain and has dealt with your mistakes. Hands that are strong enough to protect you. Hands that are tender enough to hold you lovingly.

27th April May you know the blessings of a thankful heart, a still and quiet spirit, and a peaceful mind. Whatever you are walking through now, and whatever you face tomorrow, may God the Father be your guard, Christ the Son be your comfort, and the Spirit of life be your strength.

28th April May the grace of God break through the clouds of your life like a warm setting sun, reminding you that no matter how dark your day may have been, God has not abandoned you. May hope stir in your heart with the dawn, giving you courage to step into another day.

29th April May you remember that just as daylight fades where you are, it is breaking through somewhere else. Sometimes we walk through seasons that seem darker, but God has not abandoned us in them. May you discover the beautiful power of God at work in the darker days of your life.

30th April May you have grace to give your frustrations to God and leave them there. Whatever your road, may you remember that circumstances change, but God's love and grace do not. May you be given gifts of thankfulness and trust for another day. May you see the beauty of God around you.

May

1st May May restlessness be wrestled from your soul and may weariness be untethered from your body by the strong arms of Almighty God. Amid the rising and falling of the waves of your life, may you remain rooted in the reality that God is faithfully by your side.

2nd May May you be delivered from the pain of regret over what might have been, so you can embrace what is. May you have the ability to let go of the life you thought you would have, so you can enjoy the gift of the life you actually have.

3rd May Tonight may you remember that when it feels as though God has let go of your hand, He may simply be teaching you how to walk. Amid your stumbles and falls, may you know that your Father is close at hand, and through everything, He will finish what He has started in you.

4th May May you be comforted to know that those you love are held by God's gracious hand; you can lay your burdens and worries for them at God's feet. Remember that His hands are stronger than yours: He knows them, loves them, and is closer than their breath. You can trust Him.

5th May May you be released from sorrow, lifted from despair, delivered from fear, and guarded from anxiety. May your soul be turned toward hope, your heart open to new beginnings, your spirit set on a better future. Your story isn't finished yet, so don't write yourself off.

6th May When others' words pierce your soul, may you know God's healing as He removes their sting. When others' expectations crush you, may you know God's strength picking you up and restoring your courage. When you feel inadequate, may you be reassured of God's sufficiency.

7th May May God remind you that He is your safe harbour. Whatever gales you face, however fierce the waves might be, He has the strength and the wisdom to shield you from the storms, protect you from the wind, and cover you until the squall passes. He is your true north.

8th May Remember that the clouds do not last; they will break and the Son still shines. May you have courage to trust amid the shadows of uncertainty and trace the light and grace of God in your life day by day. He will not abandon you. He does not break His promises.

9th May May God's whispered voice bring you comfort. May a sunset and a dawn help you to remember that He moves in seasons and rhythms. May you be able to let go of the hands of those you have loved and lost, entrusting them to God's gracious tender care. May you have hope.

10th May May your security be rooted in God alone. When others hurt you, may you be given grace to leave them in the hands of Christ. When you find your life taking a turn you didn't want, may you trust that God is still there. May you find rest, peace, and acceptance in God.

11th May If childhood simplicity feels like a distant memory, may God sustain childlike faith in you. If your heart is crushed by the actions of a friend, may God help you to hope again. If a once-occupied chair beside you sits empty, may God remind you that He never leaves.

12th May May God fill your heart with a sense of possibility. May the beautiful grace of God draw you toward hope and a new beginning. May you lay all of your regrets and sorrows over what has been at His feet and embrace the outstretched hand of God for a new beginning.

13th May May God remind you that failure is not fatal. May He give you courage to let go of the mistakes you have made and to trust Him to take the broken pieces of your story and craft a mosaic of hope. Remember that failing does not mean you are a failure. You are loved.

14th May May grace be the prism through which a rainbow of love, hope, and joy is refracted across your life, bringing restoration, and may your journey see the light of God break into every moment. May your soul be stilled and may the gift of faith be received with open hands.

15th May May you grow in expectation and may cynicism wither and die in you and around you; may possibility push out complacency and your dreams burn more brightly in your soul than your memories do; may what could be become a stronger magnet than what once was. Never settle.

16th May May you be reminded of the faithful promises of God; as you look back, may you trace the threads of God's mercy, compassion, and grace like a tapestry of hope and beauty. May you remember that He walks with you and that He has been present through every storm.

17th May May you enter a season of fruitfulness, your life laden with the blossoms of God's blessing; and may your roots be deeply embedded in the grace and mercy of God. May your days be marked with thankfulness and may the fragrance of your life be heavy with hope.

18th May May you be content to know the next step without having to know the journey's end. Amid your circumstances, may you have the peace to know that you do not need to know everything. Sometimes the answers you want simply don't come. In those moments, may you trust God.

19th May May restlessness be lifted from you and replaced with peace; may sorrow not sap you, and comfort console you instead; may you be freed from fear through the gift of courage. May the seeds of faith, hope, and love be sprinkled across your soul, blossoming into life.

20th May In a broken world, may you draw near to God. He knows your worst fears, deepest questions, and darkest thoughts, and continues to offer you His hand. Trusting God can be difficult. It always takes courage. Amid your worst moments, He is still there. May you trust Him.

21st May May you discover your Creator's love through Jesus. Cling to Him and become a participant in God's great revolution of love that was birthed at the manger, secured at the cross, sustained through the resurrection, and is accessed by repentance. Grasp God's offered hand.

22nd May May you carry seeds of hope and love in your life; may they be planted in lives around you, bearing much fruit. May seeds of despair and sadness be uprooted and removed from your life. May your life bear fruit from seeds of God's promises planted deeply in your soul.

23rd May May you rest in the power and security of God's assurance and mercy. He stills the troubled soul, speaks calm into the storms of our lives, and stays with us when waves break over us. May His presence be your promise. His tenderness brings tranquillity.

24th May May your life be laden with grace, your hands heavy with the hope of God's mercy; may your steps be strengthened by God's Spirit and may tomorrow bring a sense of new beginnings, possibility, and life.

25th May May you learn the art of sitting with God, letting Him listen to your soul's cry as you listen to the heartbeat of His love. May your weariness be released as you let His rhythm become yours. He gives energy to the weary and reinvigorates them with fresh strength.

26th May There is always more to do, but you do not have to do it; may you receive the beautiful gift of contentment. You can neither save time nor stop its advance, so be blessed with the ability to rest in the "now". Leave the past in God's hands and trust the future to Him.

27th May May hope rise like an unbreakable spire in your life, your home, and your community. May you be given eyes of faith to see possibilities where others see problems, and grace where others see failure. May your words bring healing and life to the broken and vulnerable.

28th May As the moon reflects a greater light, may your life reflect God's greater grace. May you discover the freedom and possibility that comes from admitting that you do not need to be the source of life and hope. Instead you are a link to the true source, God Himself.

29th May If you feel that you are surrounded by a sea of troubles and they look as though they will overwhelm you, may you be reminded that God will give you a safe place to stand. When your heart is overwhelmed, may He lead you to the rock that is higher than the surrounding sea.

30th May May you see your life through a window of grace. May God help you to see further, dream higher, love more deeply, and trust more fully. May you see a season of growth, vibrancy, and beauty, and may you be given eyes of faith to notice the buds of hope around you.

31st May May you be deeply rooted in God's rich promises and hope, given grace to stand steady in the storm – to bend in the wind but not break. In days of sorrow and sadness, may you be held in the comfort and care of Your Creator. May you know He is always near.

June

1st June May you be given the gift of childlike trust, learning not to take yourself too seriously: the ability to smile at life's simple things, a profound belief in God's promises and goodness, and a daily ability to open your heart to others to share life and joy.

2nd June Amid the hustle and bustle of life, may you be given the gift of being still enough to remember whose you are. May you see the reflection of God's image in your life. May you be shaped by knowing that you are loved and cherished for who you are rather than what you do.

3rd June May you have grace to trust God for what lies ahead. When you cannot see around the corner, God can. Even if you cannot hear Him, He is still there. When you sense Him least, may you be given grace to rely on the deep conviction that He will never leave you.

4th June May you find a safe harbour in Christ: a shelter from the storms that rage around you; a refuge of rest from the demands and dips of life; a haven of hope in the havoc of despair; a mooring amid mourning. May you be anchored in the strength of Almighty God.

5th June May you fly higher, go further, and see more clearly than you ever have before. May you have courage to spread your wings and catch the wind of the Spirit, and may He lead you to a profound sense of freedom and possibility. May what lies ahead capture your imagination.

6th June God makes a way through your wilderness. He levels the mountains and raises the valleys to reach you and to guide you. May you be given faith for the journey, strength for the road, a sharp eye to see dangers and pitfalls, courage to keep going, and wisdom for each step.

7th June May you find hope in the cross. Look at it again, see it with fresh eyes, reflect on it. May you discover anew the love of God in Christ's death as He hung on the tree. Drink deeply from the cup of His mercy, feast upon the bread of His grace. There is life here.

8th June May you pause in a moment's beauty, thankful for it. Amid the uncertainty of what has been and might be, may you learn the gift of now: discover deep pools of God's grace and flowing waters of His love. May your life brim with hope and bear fruit in due season.

9th June May you flourish where you are planted, rooted in the love and mercy of Christ. May you experience the peace that comes from knowing that the weight of your failures has been carried by Him. Remember you have nothing to prove to anyone when you know you are loved by God.

10th June May you find balance in life – the ability to be strong when you need to be and vulnerable when necessary. May you discover the freedom that comes from the gifts of laughter and tears. May hope blaze bright in your soul. May God carry you through every trial.

11th June May grace and truth mark your soul and leave their evidence in your actions and responses. If others hurt you with false accusations and angry rumours, may you be given the ability to trust that God sees and knows all things, and your reputation is safe in His hands.

12th June As you pass through valleys where life feels hard, may you discover springs of hope and life. May God sustain you in the journey, protecting you from sharp rocks of disappointment and regret, and constantly remind you that one day you will leave the valley forever.

13th June At the stroke of a new day, may the presence and promise of Christ sustain you. May yesterday be left in God's hands. Even if you feel you could have done more, may you be able to leave it in the hands of God and turn your thoughts to tomorrow with hope and faith.

14th June May you find buds of beauty pushing through the field of daily life. When you see them, may you stop long enough to enjoy them, being still enough to be thankful. May your way be marked with mercy. May faith's fragrance linger; a perfume of promise over you and yours.

15th June May you see above the storm. Whatever you are going through, may you be given a higher viewpoint. May you remember that the clouds can hide the sunlight, but they can never destroy it. Clouds pass, storms end, and the sun never stops shining. May this bring you hope.

16th June Whatever you face, may you find grace to trust God. If you feel that your hand is outstretched in the dark, may you come to realize that God has not left you grappling with the unknown. He has come to you in the person of Christ, showing you why you can trust Him.

17th June May tomorrow be a blank page upon which God writes what is possible and helps you to dream. May you see beyond what you are facing nowadays and be given the gift of imagination, that you might dream higher, reach further, and see more clearly than you ever have before.

18th June However fragile you may feel in life or in faith, may God give you a new gift of trust, a new sense of determination, and a new resolve to stand strong. May your vulnerability become a gift of beauty that you embrace, rather than a sign of weakness that you fear.

19th June May you be held in hopefulness, your anxiety swallowed by peace, and your fear forced out by faith. May regret be replaced with possibility. May tomorrow's undiscovered encounters bring with them gifts of thankfulness and joy. May you look up with trust, not down with worry.

20th June May you find space to rest. In the midst of chaos, may it not engulf you. Surrounded by a raging storm, may you not be overcome by the wind or waves. If you face uncertainty, may it not unnerve you. Instead, may stillness guard your heart and peace protect your soul.

21ˢᵗ June May grace light your way, hope illuminate your soul, and mercy shine upon your heart. No matter how many times you have failed, may you lift your hands to God and let Him pick you up again, released from the confinement of fear and open to a new day and a fresh start.

22nd June May you find the wonder in waiting, a gift of space between what was and what is to be. May you embrace uncertainty as a gift leading to deeper trust and greater expectation. May it be treasured time, not a gap to be filled. May you notice God in the spaces of life.

23rd June May you see beauty through the hard spaces in your life. Even when you feel you have hit a wall, may you be given the grace to find a gap and see beyond your current circumstances. Remember that an obstacle doesn't change reality; it just hides it for a while.

24th June As you enter another day, may you be given the gifts of childlike faith and joy: faith to believe that you are not alone and that God is at work in your life; joy to celebrate the beauty in your life and to enter into the profound colours of hope that each dawn brings.

25th June May God hold you amid uncertainty. May fear be lifted from your heart by the warmth of His love, just like the gloaming is lifted by the heat of the rising sun. May the light of God's presence chase away shadows and may hope sustain you in the darkest moments.

26th June May you rest in the grace of God like a child sitting in the summer sun. May you be filled with hope and drained of despair. No matter how lost you may have felt, may you know the security of being found. No matter how deep your fears, may you find a deeper courage.

27th June May you rest well, knowing that everything today held is past. You cannot relive it, change it, or stay in it. May its accomplishments and joys bring thankfulness to your soul. May its mistakes and sorrows not break you. May you have fresh faith and hope for a new day.

28th June Never settle for less than God's best for you. If people hurt you, may you be given grace to trust that God cares. If you feel deceived, may you be given courage to believe that God knows. If friends forsake you, may you find comfort in knowing God has no favourites.

29th June As the heat of the day wanes and the night skies bring coolness, may you be refreshed in your own spirit. May the worries and weights of the day be lifted as you sleep, and may you rise tomorrow a little taller in yourself and a little more determined in your soul.

30th June May you turn to face the Son. In the light of His grace, may your soul open to the possibilities that hope brings. May you be reminded that tomorrow does not need to be feared. Remember that the next twenty-four hours can bring new friendships and fresh discoveries of beauty.

July

1ˢᵗ July May God still your soul. May waves be calmed, the wind hushed, and tides eased. May trouble be lifted from your spirit and replaced with peace, the choppy waters of uncertainty becoming as still as a mill pond, ripples of fear brought to an end by the gift of faith.

2ⁿᵈ July When you look up, may your life be filled with colour, patterned with possibility, endued with deep and beautiful hues of hopefulness, pregnant with patterns of purpose. May you be reminded that grace brings new beginnings and the assurance that change is possible.

3ʳᵈ July May your soul slow down a little to notice the gift of a moment, the joy of a shared smile, the beauty of a child laughing in the summer sun. May your spirit be at rest. May the demands of what screams urgency not crowd out the importance of a peaceful soul.

4ᵗʰ July May you be given grace to accept that seasons change in unique times and rhythms. If you are stepping from one season of life to another, may you know that God is there. If you have to let go of someone, something, or somewhere, may you have courage to do so gently.

5ᵗʰ July May you discover the freedom that comes from being yourself; the gift of knowing that you are loved by God with nothing to prove and no need to hide. May you be liberated from trying to win other people's approval, and live in a posture of openness and authenticity.

6ᵗʰ July May you remember that clouds break, night passes, and the light breaks through. Whatever you are facing right now, may you be given grace to hold on to the fact that God is holding on to you. Darkness doesn't get the last word in your life. Light is always stronger.

7th July May you find the gift of stillness: room to rest and to reflect; time to be thankful for what really matters in your life. As you step from the space between what was into what comes next, may you mourn what is lost and take hold of what is to be. Space still matters.

8th July Whatever valley you may be passing through, may you find a sure place for your feet and light for your path. May your eyes be lifted from the shadows and set upon the hope of God's presence. The valley does not last forever. You will walk in hope and light again.

9th July May God paint colours of kindness from a palette of possibility in your life. May you discover the vibrancy of grace, and hues of hope splashed across the canvas of your soul. May your future be filled with portraits of mercy and drawn on a landscape of love.

10th July May you have childlike joy; an ability to laugh at the simplest things of life and enjoy every moment as a gift of grace. May you be able to step away from the weight of worries, even if only for a moment, and discover treasures in thankfulness and a happy heart.

11th July May you be given a profound sense of safety. God is your defender, security, and protection. May He push out your fears, hold you amid uncertainty, comfort you in sorrow, be your calm in the noise, and put a hedge of protection around you and those you love.

12th July Tonight, may you be held in peace and grace by the One who made you and knows you. Whatever you face, may you remember that God is able to carry you through it. He will wipe every tear away, carry every burden, and listen to every sigh. He is present. He is faithful.

13th July May you have space to think, dream, and imagine. May you see beyond where you are now, and have the gift of sensing what is possible. May your current circumstances not dictate your future state. May you be given the gift of faith – often needed most when sensed least.

14th July If you have been hurt, may you trust God with the wrongdoing. If your character has been unfairly attacked, may you rely on the God who understands. If someone seems to be getting away with lies, may you remember that God knows. Trust God with wounds inflicted by friends.

15th July May you have the ability to pay attention to your own soul. May you find the right rhythm for life, learn to invest in friendships, protect relationships, and pay attention to your soul's well-being and your mental health, knowing when to say "yes" and when to say "no".

16th July If you are facing a storm, may God give you courage and determination. May He hold you through the hurricane, protect you through the gale. May He hold your ship steady as the waves crash around you. May you not only endure the assault, but also grow through it.

17th July May you embark on the next season of your life with a sense of adventure. Be inspired by what could be and not intimidated by it. May fear be put to flight. May you have the ability to find faith: worry pushed out by trust. May your smallness help you see God's vastness.

18th July May you be given the gift of purpose and not be distracted by those things that are secondary. May your heart's compass be set on Christ as its true north, never drawn off course by popularity, wealth, or position. May you be given grace to always put God first.

19th July

May tomorrow be like
a blank page. May you
discover lines yet to be written,
encounters yet to be had, thoughts
yet to be imagined, and possibilities
beyond your wildest dreams. May you
know the grace of God with every word, and
find your place in God's great story.

20th July May God paint beauty into your life in simple ways, giving you grace to notice the wonder in a moment, and an eye to see the stillness of His presence. May you find your rest in him always. As you reflect on your circumstances, may He bring peace, giving you hope.

21st July May you be given grace to lift your head in a storm and turn your eyes towards heaven. May you find courage to face your fears and humility to let God's strength strengthen you. Even if the clouds ahead of you are dark, may you allow God's light to guide your steps.

22nd July May you be thankful, seeing the gift of God in being alive. Surrounded by difficulties? May God give you space to breathe. Surrounded by joy? May you have the grace to celebrate. Facing challenges and uncertainty? May you hear His voice bringing guidance and peace.

23rd July May your day tomorrow be vibrant with joy. May you have the grace to notice things that bring a smile to your face and rejoicing to your soul. Whether you are in a valley or on a mountaintop, may you be blessed with a moment of beauty and hopefulness lifting your spirit.

24th July May God fan the embers of your life into flame. Where hope has been snuffed out, may it blaze again; where joy has died, may it burn brightly once more. Where ashes are all that remain of love once shared and dreams once held, may God bring beauty to your soul again.

25th July May you be rooted in hopefulness. May you be reminded that God's grace is strong enough to surround you through the storm. His commitment is unwavering, even when waves crash upon you. When promises are often broken, may you be tethered to His unbreakable assurances.

26th July May your soul be stilled by God's Spirit and your heart be held in hope by God's hand. May your worries be lifted and your anxieties laid down by the assurance that God is your light in the darkness, your beacon in the night, and the safe harbour you need.

27th July May God speak gently over you, whispering grace, hope, and peace. May His quiet voice be louder than the roaring doubts that assault you; may the assurance of His presence chase the darkness of fear away. Remember that you can only hear the whisper of one who is close.

28th July In the world's vastness, may you know that you are known. The One who flung the stars into space holds the universe and knows the hairs on your head, the fears that you face, and the uncertainty surrounding you. Amid the chaos, may you know the Creator's closeness.

29th July May you sleep deeply, remembering that God never slumbers. As you rest, He watches over you. As you are unaware of the world around you, He has set His angels as guards. You are never out of His sight and you are never beyond His grace, His mercy, and His protection.

30th July May you find contentment: a deep sense of being at peace within yourself. Remember that God sees your brokenness and beauty. He brings healing to our lives, and liberates us from the worst of ourselves. He sees beauty beyond our shame, offering us hope and grace.

31st July May you find life in the desert, discovering that God sustains through dry seasons. No matter how hard your situation is, remember that God can cause hope to bud. He brings beauty in barrenness, and wherever you are planted, may you remember that you can flourish.

August

1st August May you know godly surrender, your struggles becoming moments of grace. May you know that God's perspective on your sorrow can bring hope amid heartbreak and trust in turmoil. May your pain be offered to God and may His peace be received by you.

2nd August May your heart be held in the midst of anxiousness and your spirit stilled even when surrounded by uncertainty; may your concerns and cares for those you love be carried by the One who sustains you in every moment and is closer than your breath. He knows and cares.

3rd August May you find peace in waiting. May you discover that in moments between now and then, between where you long to be and where you end up, a beautiful and powerful change can take place within you that gives you courage to stand in the present with strength and hope.

4th August May you know the gift of knowing that God is near. At times when you feel alone, whatever your life's circumstances are, may you be given the gift of faith to believe that God sits with you, listens to your soul, and knows you deeply. May His company comfort you.

5th August May you know the gift of God's acceptance. You have nothing to prove to Him, nothing you need to hide from Him, and there is nothing in you that can disillusion Him. May you rest in His grace, letting your guard down before Him. Come to Him with open hands, not clenched fists.

6th August As you leave today behind, may you lay down its mistakes and sorrows, knowing that God knows all things. May you also lay down the successes and achievements of today. May you remember that neither your achievements nor your defeats define you. May God be your compass.

7ᵗʰ August May you find grace to let go. Entrust those you love into God's care. His love is stronger and His mercy deeper than ours. Whether parting for a while, nearing a final farewell, leaving friends and colleagues, or remembering someone who has gone, find grace in Christ.

8ᵗʰ August May God carry you through the night, setting a watch over your soul and protecting you. May sleeplessness be lifted and rest granted to your mind and body. May your turmoil be stilled and your worry replaced with a deep sense of peace. God Himself is your guard.

9ᵗʰ August God takes shards of a broken heart and creates a mosaic of hope. To have loved deeply and to have been loved are precious gifts. May you cherish memories of love shared and be given grace to be thankful for what you have had, not resentful at what you have lost.

10th August May your heart be held tenderly in the loving hands of God. May you rest knowing He is present; may you awaken knowing that He goes before you. Nothing that lies ahead of you is stronger than God's love – His grip is strong enough to trust.

11th August May you be given wisdom to know that your deepest longings can only be met by God and His grace. His peace is more profound than any trouble, His presence more sure than any storm. Even when you cannot see Him, He is there; when you cannot feel Him, He is holding you.

12th August May you pause on your journey, remembering that God is there. As evening, night, and morning flow into each other, may you recall that God connects the seasons of life in a tapestry of grit and grace. Amid your confusion, have hope that God holds life's threads together.

13th August May the kaleidoscope of your memories bring a glimpse of the many facets of God's grace and love. Whatever you have come through, however heartbreaking and difficult, may God bring comfort for the difficult memories and gratefulness for the good ones. Keep going!

14th August May you remember that the cross stands strong. Cultures come and go, but may the cross remind you that God still embraces the broken, forgives sin, and offers hope and new life to all who will receive God's grace through Christ. May you receive a fresh gift of faith.

15th August Remember that God does not break bruised reeds or snuff out smouldering flames. May you have fresh strength for a new day tomorrow. You are not defined by grades or what others say about you. May you have a deep sense of confidence in God's grace and purposes for your life.

16th August May you be able to see potential in tomorrow. Whatever yesterday held, may you release it to God. Whatever today has brought, may you know the freedom of learning from it but not being confined by it. May you see possibilities where others see obstacles.

17th August May God be your safe harbour – a place of peace and a defence against the storm. May His grace give you strength to face the days ahead with faith. You may not be able to predict what tomorrow will bring, but may you rest in God's promises and take refuge in Him.

18th August May God guide you through the fog. Remember that He is by your side. Even if you cannot see to put one foot in front of the other, may you have peace in your soul because God is with you – His presence is enough. May He remind you that the mist will lift. May it do so soon.

19th August Facing change, may you know God's unwavering commitment of grace and love. When uncertainty surrounds you, may you know the constancy of His care. When unpredictability leaves you feeling unsure, may the assurance of His presence and promises bring peace to your soul.

20th August May your soul be stilled by the promises of God. As you journey through this season of your life, may God's whispered assurances bring you peace and may you find comfort in God's word. He offers His hand of hope to all who will accept it through His Son Jesus.

21st August May you be set free from the compulsion for certainty. Not all questions need to be answered. May you grow into the mystery of God's grace. May your questions and uncertainties become doorways into wonder and pathways into worship of God.

22nd August May you experience hope in waiting, discovering God's presence and peace during in-between times. May you be reminded that God has more to reveal, that life has more to be discovered, and that the period between "now" and "then" does not need to be wasted or empty.

23rd August May your soul be stilled and your spirit comforted by the peace of God. May you sense the quiet beyond the noise, the calm beyond the storm, and the hope beyond your current circumstances. May God remind you that He has not finished with you. You can still trust Him.

24th August May you be given grace to "trace the rainbow through the rain". May you see colours of tenderness refracted through your tears. May the spray from the storm's waves become hundreds of hues of hope that bring skyscapes of light and peace amid your life's dark times.

25th August May sunset remind you that all that is past is gone, safe with God who holds all the threads of our lives in His hands tenderly and securely. As Earth awaits the dawn, may you hold on to the fresh mercies of God in Christ. May grace enfold you in the new day ahead.

26th August May your soul be stilled. Amid things you do not know, may you know the peace of God within: a peace that does not come through intellect. It is deeply rooted in trusting that He is good, even when life is not. May you rely on Him, even when you do not understand Him.

27th August May you face the future with hopefulness, seeing what could be and discovering glimpses of God in ordinary and everyday things. May you see His love in the seams of life, moments that we so often miss – like a stranger's smile, a child's carefree laugh, or a dawn.

28th August May you be restored by rest and find time to breathe. May grace galvanize your resolve and give you new-found determination to pursue your purpose and face another day. May you be held in the Spirit's hope, rooted in the Son's mercy, and secured in the Father's love.

29th August May you be given the gift of seeing your future as a blank canvas upon which you give God the space and time to paint possibilities. May you be given grace not to fear the blank space, but instead find the courage to be open to what could be ahead for you.

30th August May your life be laden with God's good gifts: grace for each moment, hope for the future, strength for the present, and love for a lifetime. May you be comforted in your sorrow, carried through every season, and may the fragrance of faith linger over your home.

31st August May you be given the gift of self-awareness, learning to be honest about your strengths and weaknesses and open to growth. May you discover gifts of reflection and contentment, holding the tension between true humility and not being too hard on yourself.

September

1st September May your restlessness be stilled by the peace and presence of God. May sleeplessness be lifted and a sense of calm enfold you like a blanket of comfort. May you rise to a new day tomorrow with a renewed sense of purpose and determination.

2nd September May the light of God illuminate your path and may the grace of God linger over you like a fragrance of hope. May you know, deep within your soul, that God loves you and has opened His hands toward you, offering an embrace of welcome, a heart of mercy.

3rd September May the night bring with it rest and restoration. May the day ahead bring new moments of grace and hope. May your soul be strengthened by the Spirit of God to face the future with faith and fortitude.

4th September May your mistakes become moments of grace, in which you allow God to mark you with His mercy and repair your soul with His tender hand. May you experience the beauty of a teachable spirit, learning to be open to new things, seeing faith grow from your failures.

5th September At the end of another day, may you be given the gift of trust. Amid unexpected heartbreak and unwanted sadness, may you be given grace to reach out your hand to Almighty God and give Him the last twenty-four hours. He has already reached out His hand to you in Christ.

6th September May you have grace to let go, entrusting those you love to the hands and purposes of God. May you be given gifts of memory, to recall the many good things and precious moments in your life. May you be given the ability to love people tightly but hold them lightly.

7th September May you be blessed through the gift of kindness. May you experience it through the overwhelming mercy and patience of God and through the gentleness and generosity of others. May you demonstrate it to others too, treating them as you would want God to treat you.

8th September May you have grace to leave the failures of the past behind; may you have the humility to let God be your strength in the present; and may you have faith to believe that He will not abandon you tomorrow. May your heart be set on Him always.

9th September May you allow yourself space and time to adjust to new seasons; be kind to yourself, allow moments to reflect and remember. May your heart overflow with gratitude for what has been, and may you step into what is next with a sense of anticipation and hopefulness.

10th September May you walk in the grace of gratefulness. May you experience the blessing of being thankful for those around you and the gifts you enjoy, and may you also be blessed by the thankfulness of another toward you, helping you to feel that you are not taken for granted.

11th September May you have a spirit of adventure with the courage to step into a new chapter of your story bravely and in faith. Courage is not the absence of fear; it is being determined to step into the unknown with a sense of dependence on God despite your uncertainties.

12th September Sometimes our lives feel like a state of perpetual waiting: for the next change, the next door to open, the next crisis to pass, the next possibility to unfold. May you find grace and peace in waiting, learning to trust God in the moments between "now" and "then".

13th September May your soul's compass be held in the direction of Christ and His grace. Even when the news you hear is heartbreaking and the waves rage around you, trying to pull you off course, may God continually be your magnetic north. May He hold your gaze amid the storms.

14th September May your heart be held securely in the hands of hope. May your soul be shielded from the shattering storms of sadness. May you be given the grace to know that God knows what you face and He will carry you through it. May you hear Him whisper peace to your heart.

15th September May you discover the possibilities that come through prayer. Whether your cry to God is whispered in worship or exhaustion, uttered in conviction or longing, or declared in determination or desperation, may you experience God's nearness and the power of His promises.

16th September May you be given peace of mind: the weight of worry lifted by the strong hand of God; the uncertainty of tomorrow somehow held at bay by the guarding presence of Christ. Whatever lies ahead, may God give you courage to keep trusting throughout fear's onslaught.

17th September May you breathe fresh air tonight, and as you do, may you exhale the regrets, disappointments, and frustrations of the day that has been and inhale a sense of life and grace. May you open the window of your soul to God's mercy, sensing the scent of hope in your spirit.

18th September May you discover that your soul's longings can only be satisfied when they are set on the lavish love of God. May you never settle for secondary satisfactions. Instead, may you discover the joy, peace, and stability that flow from God being your centre and your hope.

19th September May peace pervade your soul; may the arms of grace enfold you; may the love of God surround you; and may hope hold you in its grip no matter what you face, how you feel, or what today has brought.

20th September When far from those you love, may you be given comfort in the absence, and grace to remember moments of tenderness shared, gifts of friendship, love and family. May you be given companions for your journey in life who will walk with you through every season.

21st September May you be given space to count your blessings. Despite whatever challenges you face and whatever heartbreaks you are enduring, and no matter what uncertainties and trials you are going through, may the gift of thankfulness lift your soul and strengthen your peace.

22nd September May you sense stillness after the storm; may the rays of grace reflect on the deep, mysterious waters of sorrows and struggles, bringing beauty to the surface like refractions of hope. God's light enables you to see through darkness, like light bouncing off the moon.

23rd September May you leave the labours of the day with God, knowing that He can take the seeds you have sown and bring much fruit from them. May you give Him your moments of victory and celebration, as well as your moments of failure and disappointment. What's done is done.

24th September May you be given grace to root your view of yourself and others in the fundamental reality that we are each made in God's image and loved by Him. May you be liberated from categorizing yourself or others too quickly, dismissing unkindly, or jumping to conclusions.

25th September May you follow signposts of love and grace that point you toward life. May God's words bring truth that liberates you. May the kindness and compassion of Christ bring hope to your soul. May the Spirit's presence and power strengthen your sense of belonging and purpose.

26th September May God's grace increase your capacity to be gracious; may God's love lead to a deeper love in your soul for others; may the gift of hope help you to share hopefulness with others; and may God's mercy leave its mark on your life, making you merciful to those you meet.

27th September May God comfort you in your sorrow and carry you through unexpected heartbreaks. When you reach the end of yourself, and feel lost and confused, may God take your hand and lead you through the fog. May you be given grace to give God your pain and confusion.

28th September May you be given strength to endure the trial. When you feel you cannot keep going, may you discover God's strength sustaining you, God's closeness comforting you, and God's promises reminding you that this too will pass. Your sorrow is not eternal.

29th September As waves crash upon you, your anchor holds. As darkness tries to terrorize you, be reminded that dawn always breaks. As you feel pain and heartbreak in saying "goodnight", may you find hope as you remember that one day you will say "good morning", never to be parted again.

30th September Whatever is going on in your life, may you know a deep peace – your heart tuned to heaven's music. At times, the melody of our souls changes to the minor key of sorrow. In those moments, may the key change bring depth and not despair. There is beauty amid the pain.

October

1st October When it feels as though God's timing is forcing you out of your rhythm, may you be given grace to adjust your life to fit His rhythm. When your days are disrupted by unexpected, and even unwelcome events, may you receive faith to keep trusting that God is still present.

2nd October May you find strength in your weakness, hope in the midst of despair, and peace when surrounded by trouble. May you discover life, even when confronted by death, and be given the gift of trust in the face of uncertainties. May you learn to walk in the paradox of faith.

3rd October When you come to the end of yourself, may you find there is more of God. When you feel your life has hit a wall of despair, may God's grace break through, giving you room to breathe and space to move. May your memories bring joy and gratitude as an antidote to grief.

4th October May God's silent presence drown out the world's noise around you. May the reality of His hand upon you give a profound grace and personal sense of security in an uncertain world. May He beautify your trial, causing hope to blossom and faith to grow in the desert.

5th October As one season gives way to another, may you walk in trust, live in hope, and wait with expectation. As autumn colours glow in the evening sun, may you trust that new life will come as old life fades away, the morning sun bringing fresh anticipation and a new beginning.

6th October May you open your hands to receive strength for the days ahead. May sleep reorder your thoughts as God refreshes your body, mind, and soul. May the weight of your sorrows be lifted, the resolve of your will guarded, and your ability to endure the trial strengthened.

7th October May you know God close in absence. He understands your deepest fears and darkest moments. He walks through valleys with you, even the shadow of death. Just as shadows break in the light of the risen sun, so your despair will be scattered by the risen Son in the end.

8th October May hope hold you fast. Facing uncertainty, may you be given strength, guarded by grace and protected by God's presence. May His anchor keep you steady and safe in the storm. God is your safe harbour.

9th October May fear's threats be silenced by hope's promises. May the terror of darkness be destroyed by the presence of light. May the nausea of uncertainty be settled by the giver of faith. Fragility is not weakness. Honesty is not failure. Hope requires no pretence.

10th October May God bestow the gift of hope upon your mind, hands, and heart. Remember that hope is embodied in a person; it is not an idea, a philosophy, or a concept. Hope has a name: Jesus – the resurrected, faithful One. He breaks fear, vanquishes death, and is always here.

11th October May you find grace to stand in hope, and courage to be a voice of hope to those around you. May you see possibility in your own life and in the lives of others. If things look impossible, may God give you grace to see further. It isn't over until He says so.

12th October May you remember that the hope brought to the world by Christ can never be extinguished. No tyranny is strong enough, no evil is great enough to overcome Christ's hope in us. May you be held in hope's hands: a nail-pierced, tender, yet unbreakable grip.

13th October Just as night passes and the morning dawns, so may you be reminded that hope will push back fear. May the strong, eternal purposes of God shape you. Do not believe the lie that this is as good as it gets. Hope has the last word because God has the final say.

14th October Surrounded by uncertainty, may hope hold open the door of trust. May the light of Christ lead you on, illuminating your steps and preventing you from stumbling. It is enough to take one step at a time, celebrating each small victory and trusting for the next.

15th October May God breathe His peace upon you.
May you experience His stillness in your soul, even
if the storms rage around you. May your heart be
shielded from fear, shalom saturating your spirit.

16th October May the peace of God pervade your
soul: the promise of God's presence permeating every
part of you, stilling your soul, assuaging your anxieties,
and removing your restlessness. May you be given
faith to see through your current circumstances, and
see that God sees you.

17th October May you be reminded tonight that
God's peace is indivisible from His presence. Just as
He promises you that He will never leave you when
you commit your life to Him, so He promises that His
peace is your portion. May you cling to the God who
clings to you.

18th October May God break the dam of fear that blocks the flow of peace; may He scatter the clouds of uncertainty that hide the light of His Son. If you are drenched by the rain of anxiety, may the light of God's presence be refracted into a rainbow of hope and peace.

19th October May you discover that peace is not passive, but active. It guards your soul, calms your fears, holds you steady, protects your heart, and galvanizes your resolve. May you walk in peace and step into tomorrow with single-minded purpose and godly determination.

20th October May you learn to breathe, each inhalation infusing peace. Exhale the stresses and strains of the day, letting its dissonance disappear into the past. Breathe in life for the next moment, because each second is sent to be savoured. Find peace in the present.

21st October May you know peace that comes from God, and stillness that comes from the Saviour. May you be held by the gaze of the Son of God, just as He must have held His mother's gaze. May stillness and hope, secured in the Christ-child, be experienced in your soul tonight and always.

22nd October May you discover a joy that is deeper than sorrow, rooted not in your circumstances but in your Creator and His commitment to you. May you lean into God's joy over you, letting it become your strength.

23rd October May you find grit to guard joy, because sometimes you have to fight to protect it. No one can take it from you without your permission, so may you be able to make tough decisions to shield it. Sin starves joy of breath, so may you resist sin and breathe in joy.

24th October As night falls, may joy blaze brightly in your heart. May you remember that sorrow has been swallowed by comfort, fear has been overcome by faith. In your honesty and openness, may joy take root and grow. May you shelter under the branches of God's grace.

25th October May joy nourish and sustain you, and flow in your soul. Receive the gift of thankfulness, so you can find things to be grateful for in each moment. May the weight of worry be replaced with a mantle of praise. Even in the valley of tears, may you find a spring.

26th October May grace be like an eruption of joy in your soul. In Christ, your sins are forgiven and your shame is removed. May the rumour rise in your soul, the whispered voice of God drowning out the silence. He has come to you! Allow Him to embrace you in His grace.

27th October May the life-giving, soul-strengthening, hope-building gift of joy be yours tonight in abundance. In the midst of the darkest moments, may the joy of the Lord be a light for you. Surrounded by uncertainty, may you sing for joy at the faithfulness of God.

28th October May you hear rumbles of celebration. In the stillness of the air, hear myriad angels' voices begin to celebrate the Saviour. The message rings above rumbles of broken hearts, shattered dreams, and sorrow's tears. God has come to us. That changes everything.

29th October May love uphold you deeply in every way. For the broken, He brings wholeness; for the lonely, He brings friendship; for the mourning, He brings comfort. May the dark clouds scatter and God's love shine in your soul. Love has a name: Jesus. He has come near.

30th October God has come among us. May this truth bring courage and joy to your soul. No matter what you face, God stretches His hands toward you in embrace, and promises to transform darkness and break chains of despair. You are not alone. May you receive God's life and hope.

31st October May you receive the gift of faith with the same honesty and vulnerability as Mary, when she heard that she would bear God's Son. May Christ be birthed in you and trust deepened. Step into the future, your eyes fixed on God's promises and purpose.

November

1st November May you discover that God takes you further when you trust Him for each step. What brought you "here" may not get you "there", but God gives fresh grace for every moment, fresh vision for every dawn, and fresh gifts for every situation. May you trust Him as you travel.

2nd November May you walk with faith in the life you have and not yearn for the idealized life you wanted. May you have space to lay down unrealistic expectations, and faith to embrace the beauty and power of the life that you are in. May you find rubies hidden on life's road.

3rd November May you be strengthened by God's grace to face uncertainty with courage, fear with faith, and disappointment with hope. May you remember that God is more faithful than anyone you will ever know and more loving than you could ever imagine. May His comfort surround you.

4th November May you be strengthened for tomorrow. Whatever the battle might be, God is strong enough to defend and protect you; wherever you are, God is there too; no matter what you face, God can bring you through it. May His closeness comfort you and His strength sustain you.

5th November May you be given the ability to see the thread of grace in your story. No matter how complicated, dark, or painful your life has been, may God enable you to find strands of hope. Amid the tapestry of challenges, may you find shades of strength and trust.

6th November Each day brings its own challenges and choices. May you be given grace to make good choices: faced with uncertainty, choose trust; when experiencing doubt, choose faith; when walking through conflict, choose peace-making; when faced with the dark, wait for the dawn.

7th November May mercy mark your moments and love lead you home. May you be reminded that grace is greater than shame, and forgiveness stronger than bitterness. May God guard your soul.

8th November May your heart be softened by sorrow and not hardened; your spirit strengthened and not crushed; your soul find peace and not anxiety. As you walk in the shadows of uncertainty, may the presence of God alongside you give you hope because He is with you.

9th November Just as night passes and the morning dawns, so may you be reminded that hope will push back fear. May the strong, eternal purposes of God shape you. Do not believe the lie that this is as good as it gets. Hope has the last word, because God has the final say.

10th November When anxiety makes you feel as though you cannot breathe, may God remove its grip on your soul and give you peace. When fear tries to extinguish the light of hope in your life, may God remind you that He does not snuff out a flickering flame. May His Spirit be your shield.

11th November May you know that you are loved more deeply than you could ever imagine. In your brokenness, fragility, uncertainty, and imperfections, know that you are known. Beyond cards, flowers, and gifts, your worth is seen in what God has given for you: His life.

12th November May your eyes be open to what might be, and may you be given a fresh gift of faith for this season of your life. May you embrace possibility over fear and hope over despair. May your disappointments be swallowed by the promise of God. He will finish His work in you.

13th November Life is marked by mystery, laced with grace. Pause in the moments when things do not make sense, to be reminded that a stronger hand rests on the tiller of your days. May you learn the art of reorientation – letting God shape you and give you definition as you travel on.

14th November We are not guaranteed another dawn. We do not know what tomorrow will bring. May you grasp the moments you are given, to live well, love deeply, and pursue choices that will help you to look back on your day with a sense of gratefulness and free from regret.

15th November Our souls were fashioned to worship God. His melody resonates deep in our spirits like a lost song that we yearn to sing, but somehow we have forgotten the notes and lyrics. May you discover this anthem of grace again, and may you sing it with all you've got.

16th November Don't give up. No matter how high the bar, how difficult the challenge, or how complicated the issue, don't quit. When conversations are awkward, honesty is uncomfortable, or authenticity brings vulnerability, don't walk away. May God give you courage to hold on.

17th November May you remember that in God you have a safe harbour: a secure and protected place in the storm. May you stay close to Him through the wind and the rain. The storm will pass, the waves will still, and God will hold you fast.

18th November May you be given the gift of hope: able to see the first trace of dawn in the darkness, hear birdsong break the silence of night, and feel the warmth of the sun as morning breaks. May the promise of God's nearness swallow the uncertainty of His felt absence.

19th November May God strengthen you in body, mind, and spirit. Rest deeply in the embrace of your Creator, the One who made you, renewing and refreshing you. May your anxieties be absorbed by the giver of wisdom and grace; your spirit soothed by the Prince of Peace.

20th November May God displace despair, hold you in hope, unravel knots in your stomach, still storms in your emotions, and protect your peace. May fear fall at the empty tomb, and the Saviour's words be seeds in your heart's soil: "Be of good cheer. I have overcome the world."

21st November May God give you grace. When you come to the end of yourself, may you discover that God is always enough. When you feel imprisoned by fear, may God break open the cell and give you freedom. When your heart is broken, may God restore it, gracing you with peace.

22nd November May God give you courage. May He help you see the things you face through His eyes and not just your own. Remember that in your weakness, God is strong; in your restlessness, He is your peace; in the absence, He is there; in your lack, He is enough.

23rd November May wells of gratitude be unblocked in you, releasing refreshing waters of gratefulness. May you have the ability to notice blessings amid challenges; hopefulness amid uncertainty. May appreciation drive out apprehension in your soul.

24th November May God remind you that He is mindful of you. May you experience the One who crafted you carrying you. May the One who gives you breath hold your gaze. May the voice that spoke creation into being whisper your name. May the God of grace comfort you always.

25th November May God lift your gaze toward heaven and may you hear His whisper. May you be reminded of the things He has done rather than the things He has not. May your heart be protected from negativity and fear. May you be given grace to keep trusting.

26th November In your weakness, may you discover God's strength. In your uncertainty, may He release the gift of faith within you. In your questions, God is enough and the satisfaction of your longings. In your limited perspective, He is the gift of greater insight.

27th November May God calm the storms within your soul: the raging uncertainties, the negative voices, the hurtful words, the nagging doubts, the lurking fears, and the unspoken anxieties. May you find the steely strength of stillness, peace, and calm.

28th November May you be satisfied in God alone. Whatever your circumstances are, may you be able to lift your gaze toward heaven. Your joy need not be the source of your peace, and your despair need not deny your hope. May God Himself be your calm in the storm.

29th November May you enjoy a redeemed imagination: the ability to recall precious life-giving moments from what has been, the capacity to call to mind the good and leave aside the bad, the grace to find treasures of thankfulness buried in the story of your life.

30th November Through the ebb and flow of life, may you discover that God is your constant. He holds you in the changing seasons of life. His grace is like an anchor in the shifting sands beneath you. No matter what else changes, may you remember today and always that God's gaze is on you and His hands are open toward you in an embrace of love.

December

1st December

"Sages, leave your contemplations"

"Angels from the Realms of Glory", James Montgomery

May you discover that you do not need to understand God to trust Him. May the joy and beauty of God's mystery release deeper expectation and hope in your soul. May explanation give way to encounter for you.

2nd December

"Light of lights!
All gloom dispelling"

St Thomas Aquinas

May you be given great comfort and strength from this unshakeable truth: the light of Christ shines brightly in the darkness. Nothing can ever destroy it. This Advent, may the glorious light of God shine in you and through you.

3rd December

"As the watchers wait the dawn"
(Based on Psalm 130:6)

Look with eager eyes for the new sunrise. May you
be able to keep hoping and trusting. No matter how
long the night may be, and no matter how deep the
darkness, may God remind you that morning dawns
and darkness flees away – always.

4th December

"Watching, waiting for You,
Created and Eternal meet,
Rescue arrives."

Malcolm Duncan

This Advent, may you remember that Christ's birth gives us a Saviour. His death makes forgiveness possible. His resurrection can banish fear. His promised return means hope can be grasped.

5ᵗʰ December

"The King shall come when morning dawns
And light triumphant breaks."

"The King shall Come when Morning Dawns", Anon

May God give grace: strength to the weak, comfort to the troubled, hope to the despairing, and courage to those who are afraid. May God plant faith in your soul like a seed. You are never alone.

6ᵗʰ December

"O come, Thou Day-Spring, come and cheer
Our spirits by Thine advent here."

"O Come, O Come Emmanuel", Anon

God give you grace to pause, your gaze lifted to the star of hope; your heart softened by the holy family's devotion, bowing before the grand miracle. God came to us and will never leave.

7th December May you know the joy of the gift of Christ. He comes to those who will receive Him; He reaches out His arms to those who will let Him embrace them. True freedom comes from knowing you need a Saviour, and joy comes from accepting God's beautiful love for you.

8th December

"In the stillness of your soul
Remember the mystery of the
Christmas message;
The creator in a cradle."

Malcolm Duncan

May the starlit sky remind you of the Saviour. Hands that hold stars were pierced for you. God who upholds all things by His powerful word whispers your name as only a Father can.

9th December

*"And now my heart cannot contain,
All that my words cannot explain."*

"Immanuel, O Immanuel", Graham Kendrick © 1988

May the incarnation draw you beyond explanation into worship. May the simple message that God became human move you from a sense of isolation to God's companionship.

10th December

*"Trace we the Babe, who hath
retrieved our loss."*

"Christians Awake, Salute the Happy Morn", John Byron

May you receive the gift of faith, unlocking shackles of despair and throwing wide prison doors of sin. See the manger through the cross, and the cross through the empty tomb. Love triumphed. Hope is here. Hallelujah!

11ᵗʰ December

"Love indestructible in frailty appears."

"Meekness and Majesty", Graham Kendrick © 1986 Thankyou Music

May the Christ-child's vulnerability demolish your defences. May the cries of the babe in the Bethlehem air echo in the chambers of your heart, and the swaddling clothes of the infant Jesus remind you of the majesty He left for you.

12ᵗʰ December

Ponder the Christ child: before His human voice was heard, His word upheld things, bringing comfort to all who are broken. May you experience a word of promise spoken into your soul by Jesus. May His incarnation be your inspiration, His invitation your salvation and His love your liberation.

13th December

"So in this moment I wait. I wait."

Malcolm Duncan

May you know the profound truth that God never disappoints. He may do or permit what you do not want or understand, but may you remember that waiting is never wasted. May He give you an unshakeable hope in His love and grace.

14th December

"You took all my guilt and shame."

"You Laid Aside your Majesty", Noel Richards © 1985 Thankyou Music

May you know the utter exhilaration that comes from God's love. Lift your head to the Son and let the breeze of the Spirit blow away any fear, despair, or sense of worthlessness. You are treasured, loved, accepted, and forgiven.

15th December

"Oh rest beside the weary road,
And hear the angels sing!"

"It Came upon a Midnight Clear", Edmund Hamilton Sears

May the weights you bear be lifted by God's grace.
May you know the strength of the Spirit replacing your
weariness with energy. May you find rest, joy, and
hope in Christ. May the incarnation bring you life.

16th December

"What I can I give Him,
Give him my heart."

"In the Bleak Midwinter", Christina Rossetti

May you know the joy and expansiveness of your
life laid down for Christ. May you find grace to kneel
before the One who gave up everything for us, holding
your hands open before Him with all you are and have.

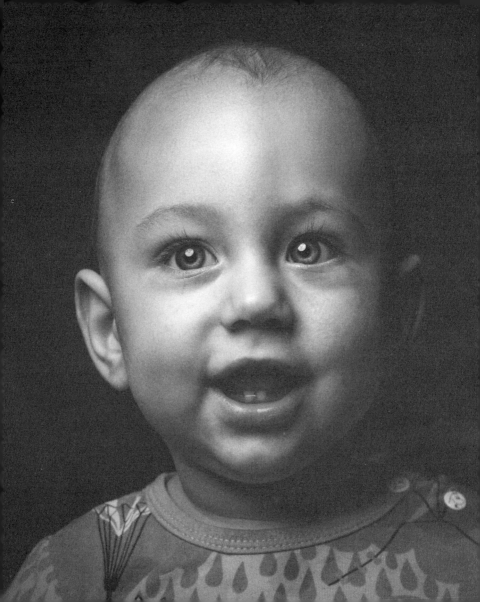

17ᵗʰ December

*"Uncreated light shines through
    infant eyes.
God is with us Alleluia."*

"The Candle Song", Graham Kendrick © 1988

May you remember that God sees you and loves you.
In His gaze, may you discover comfort, tenderness,
and love. May the uncreated light from His eyes be
a lamp for your feet and a light for your path.

18ᵗʰ December

*"Earth stood hard as iron,
Water like a stone."*

"In the Bleak Midwinter", Christina Rossetti

May Christ's coming expand your hope and deepen
your joy. Earth's very fabric is changed by this miracle.
The God who makes all things new is remaking your
life. Let fear flee and weariness wane, for Christ has
come!

19th December
"Very God, begotten not created."
"O Come All Ye Faithful", John F. Wade

May the God who whispered creation into being remind you that He was there the moment you entered the world and He will be there when you take your last breath. He constantly upholds you and is closer than you could hope.

20th December May God grant you profound joy, deep rest, and a wonderful sense of hope. May He remind you that weeping lasts for a night, but joy comes in the morning.

21st December May the rumbling anticipation of Christmas celebrations cause you to open your heart and life expectantly to God. May the invasion of the incarnation inspire you to deeper faith and greater hope. May the comfort of Christ caress your soul and bring you strength.

22nd December Christ is the thought, seed, promise, hope, and sustainer. May the thought become a seed in your life; may the seed be planted in your soul as a promise; may the promise grow in your heart and birth hope; and may hope be your sustainer always.

23rd December May the whisper of hope begin to rise in your soul. The long-awaited dawn is near. May you be given grace to wait for the arrival of a new day. May the sorrows that have weighed you down be released into the open arms of the God who has pierced the darkness, broken the silence, and come to you in the eyes of a child.

24th December On Christmas Eve, after all the chaos of the day, may you find order. After all the mess, may you find holiness. After all the noise, may you find stillness. In the face of rejection, may you find acceptance. In the midst of darkness, may the light of the world shine upon you.

25th December After the Christmas joy and celebration, may you know God's comfort if you sorrow and His presence if you feel alone. God not only became human for us, He also endured the sharpest edges of our lives, offering transformation of tears and heartbreak, for all who will receive it.

26th December May the deep and settled peace of God rest upon you and abide within you tonight and always. As the initial excitement of Christmas passes, may you be given the grace to experience the contentment that comes from knowing God is close enough to hear your sighs.

27th December May the God of life breathe fresh energy into your soul. In this Christmas season, as you await the revelation of Epiphany, may He ease your restlessness, strengthen your faith, and sharpen your focus. May He give you new passion and daily grace.

28th December May you be given the gift of remembering God's faithfulness. As you reflect at this year's end, may you see the Father's fingertips and hear the whisper of the ever-present Spirit. May you leave regret and sorrow behind, and enter the new year with hope, faith, and peace.

29th December May you be given the gift of recollection – able to let go of things that no longer matter, learn from your journey across the last twelve months, and be reminded of those things that really do matter. May you recollect the moments of this year and trace the mercy of God deeply in them.

30th December May the possibilities of what lies ahead be greater in your imagination than the regrets of what lies in your past. In the closing of the year, may the promise of God to His people echo across your heart: *"The former things have passed away... Behold I make all things new."*

(Revelation 21:4-5, ESV)

31st December May the new year's dawn lift your eyes to the horizon that lies ahead of you, as yet undiscovered. May you be given the courage to take your gaze from your current shores of familiarity and safety, and set your eyes on what might be, leaving sorrow and sadness behind.

Photo credits

**All images sourced from Unsplash
(https://unsplash.com)**